for my mother
who started me off

Acknowledgments

Poems in this collection have previously been published in the following periodicals: *The SHOp*, *Southword*, the *Stony Thursday Book*. 'Men of the South' won second prize in the Don Goodwin Poetry Award, University of Wisconsin-Milwaukee in 2000. 'Learning Irish near Ballyferriter' appeared in the anthology *Breacadh*, and 'Asylum Seekers' in *A Safe Harbour*.

Many thanks to: Jessie and Siobhán, to James Harpur for his detailed comments, to Pat Cotter and the Munster Literature Centre, Kate Kennelly, and Ann Luttrell, to Michael and my father, and also to Grainne, Eithne, Cathleen and Cathy for their support and forbearance.

The author gratefully acknowledges The Arts Council of Ireland for a bursary in 2000, and the director, administrator and staff of Hawthornden Castle for a fellowship in 2006.

For the Cosmos, time is revolving movement;
for man time is destruction.

Hermes Trismegistus, *Hermetica*

Contents

Copper Mines, Allihies

The hills
combed with tunnels,
whose walls leak
peacock blue, emerald green,
while gaping below you
is the terrifying cavern
like a great mouth,
trying to suck you in,

then
you might (cupping
your hands to conceal
surrounding country) gaze
just at the stone chimney
tipped with brick,
until clouds passing
make it seem to move
as if it were
the stone funnel of a ship...

Visiting The Book of Kells
in the Trinity College Library

At first you see almost nothing;
then letters, tumbling down the shelves,
a high dark nave, light on the old spines
umbered gold, on either side
the pale bowed heads of philosophers.
A harp set with stones has the burned
tracery of interweaving on the shaft.
In the uneven, ancient glass trees flicker by;
I spell out 'Carolus Secundus,' pass
the close-written text of a manuscript,
Synge's photographs, an old map of Paris.

A new chamber holds the treasure of the place.
Copies anaesthetize the eyes: to see
clearly you must cleanse them, start again.
The dimness of it! as if dipped in tea,
or old varnish – even to look at it
requires patience, the eye making out
only a little at a time. You might follow
the twists and whorls like a maze
but there is no ending, the thread
strays, wavers but remains the same;
only we, following the path, are changed.

High Country

You remember these places exist
by looking at old maps
so long unopened
they crack and seem to fade
at the touch;

shackled too long
to a trip on a Sunday afternoon,
today I have run away
to a land between being and nothingness
where lyre-birds play,

have left behind
grey hutches
which break the souls
of young girls and men,
and taking Fitz's old bohereen,

a pot-bellied tower signals my Waterloo,
the trainline levels the hillside
and all signs
point back to the city
but I go the other way

and emerge from bog-girt plains
to the shock of snow-covered hills
on a day when snow was immanent.
At Bweeng, a barn
of a church, and a great crucifix

shepherding the dead,
then, by a little road, 'NAD 3'.
I reverse to read the sign again:
Nead an Fhiolar Mor – the great eagle's nest –
the fuschia's russet twigs

pick out the snowed-up road
by farms precise as Breughel,
and two standing stones
left of a sharp bend
mark the beginning of this country:

the monotony of forestry
is a barrier I must not hesitate to cross
until the land,
snow-silvered, miraculous,
makes my dog mad

so she toboggans for joy,
frisking and sniffing,
rolling the scruff of her neck
till she is half black dog,
half white snow.

That this might be my kingdom.
Snow fell
but the ivy on the roofless cottage
sheltered us,
as I gazed

through the window gap
at flakes that veiled
mountain field and slope
and imagined
this the view, this my house

as I sat, ageing and content;

a few flakes of plaster on the stone
hinting at a lost whitewashed room,
faint as my clinging hope.
But dreams pass.

I headed back,
pausing only in a shielded spot –
as dogs mark land –
to leave a print of myself in the snow,
wasted and eloquent.

Between Bweeng and Nad, Autumn

The chattering twigs
of a low willow bush,
coarse mountain grass
beginning to purple:
climbing through tufts of it
that sometimes reached my waist
I avoided spearing gorse,
striking up
to the bare and heathery summit
which birthed great
clouds that drifted
above and eastwards;

swifts chattered,
the far mountains
were baubles;

the blue-mauve
of heather confused me,
making closeness seem
as though you gazed into
the heart of distance.

Journey

I

As partings must come
sooner or later
accordingly I took the train
and you the bus
along the same route,
thinking that so
our paths might be
parallel, but not touch;

a hillock bared its chalk inside
and I remembered
the cuckoo under the hill,
the horse skull
at the turn of the path
in the cattle-less bog,

as my terrifying train
set a whole fieldfull
of cattle cantering –
there was the evidence of
my shoe with traces of bog-dirt,
in the distance
the twin tips of the Paps –

until, almost at your stop,
your bus racing along the road
met us precisely on a bridge,
and, as my train
pulled out from under it,
I did not expect, suddenly,
that I would feel your loss so much.

II

On one side, the street,
on the other, the mountain,
the train pauses,
rain suddenly falls,
a blackbird is singing –

and even the name
the woman speaks on the train
is yours, as are
the bones of trees
left lying by the track,

a bulldozer
exhausted by a pile of them,
a trench filled with water,
the sky caught in it –
who provided

that freak day of sunshine
to circle us on the bog? –
when I wanted to beguile you,
see your face break
into its slow smile.

Landscape with Lovers

The power of wind
in the place, the bright light
bleaching the sky;

rutted tracks
that held nuggets of quartz,
sapphire pools;

our touching lips
seemed part of
the force of place

but it was cold,
the dog barked
implacably.

When we joined
like horses,
like paired birds,

I thought seed would
cobweb my hair, make it
ray out with stiffness,

but he saved it,
sowing a dark chasm
with riches.

The Site

As the last gold light
shivers through saplings
an unutterable peace descends.

The ruins which
we might someday make a house
are covered with forgiving leaves;

it is never lovelier than when
light lies on fresh green sward
across the end field just before night
beyond the black-boughed arch of the well,

so many birds singing,
so many leaves reach up,
so many grasses shivering in the breeze of evening,

so much light filling the porcelain sky,
so many places
the last gold light still touches –

who would need music
when the birds
and the grasses sing?

Who would leave listening, to work?

Walking in Winter

The dry leaves
were frost-fretted, cracked,
but life lurked
in the tightly-folded buds,

it was a sign
for all the nobodies
that walked this path
all that will walk it.

A heron sloped past
the sun was an epiphany
that burst out
after we had scaled the steps

and dazzled us
when we walked into the haze
where only river stones stood out
and the lit stems of dry grass;

we never spoke –
as ice, almost an inch thick,
held all evening
in the shadowed parts.

The Fisherman

So many seedlings
along the foresters' path,
sycamore, alder, the fine spears of willow,
enough to make a forest
if they were let grow long enough

and under the pinewood dark
some stems of hazel
a traveller had cut, and then left.
To walk beside water is quietening:
I gazed into the river

at another brown world underneath,
and though beer cans
and burned patches of ground
warned me not to walk alone,
why should I not travel this heaven?

Bluebells were a haze under trees,
a duck lifted suddenly from the stream –
and then I saw him,
a dark figure, unshaven,
resentful that I had broken his solitude,

and though the dogs barked
I was afraid, but walked on until
I was sure he had not followed,
until the flowers, river,
branching hazel almost distracted me,

yet where two rivers met
there was torn plastic
draped over a log in mid-stream
and even though
level waters glittered

and birds sang on,
the knowledge
I had to pass him a second time
was making me edgy,
as I looked into the water again

wondering what lurked
under the dark brown
shadow of a stone,
and if he feared women,
and had to keep them down.

Then I lifted a stick
heavy enough for a weapon
and passing the place again
saw that he had not stirred
from a rod he had in the water

and that all I had thought about him
was false, or about another.
As I walked back to the clearing
and sun glittered on the leaves,
the forest was Eden again, nearly.

Learning Irish near Ballyferriter

The reek of cattle,
the invisible larks
churning their high song out,
a raft of seabirds
lifts from the beach as I approach
the wilderness of stone and water.

It was not lifting the stones
made them beautiful
but the light as they lay, heaped;
a pod like a giant thumb
or the squirl of a worm
on a great stone warm as milk.

And the waves were mountains
scaling the jagged rock,
or glass-green walls
that rose, tottered and crumbled.
Ag dul amach: the ghosts
that fill our consciousness,

the dreams that we live out daily
or try to live out, all of us;
a rock like a crouched animal waits,
the mountains orchestrate tone upon tone,
birds are a soft close presence
that flit from hedge to field, field to hedge.

Isteach: the stillness behind
the double glazing, the dog
a heap of wrinkled fur in the kitchen;
ruined candles lean after the millenium,
an empty magnum,
pretend lives in the pub;

and then the church, boat-hull-shaped,
light piercing the dark
powerful as ever,
and to the right as we pass
a boat hull on the mountain,
bleached white.

Margaret

Little bird-bones, though
you were weak, cruelly shaped,
still your leaving this world
was a shock I found hard to accept.
Perhaps because you worked, lazed,
troubled me like the rest.
Only, after a half hour
dabbing your page with colour
you would lay your head
on the desk, fall asleep.

Prisoner

Class after class
in faded monochrome
he painted
not flowers, but
the shadow of roses.

Entering Newgrange

Willow sways
below the gardens
and true bird song mingles with false,
which are we to desire,
the real place on the windy hilltop
or the simulated, under neon and glass,
with stone pillars machined
to an exactness they could never have
achieved in the Neolithic?

Low ground
is a wilderness
it would not have been
when the builders lived there,
beyond it a bus driver berates
a tourist who has lost his ticket,

then the great mound
studded with sunstones,
seeded with dry, burnt bones;
a hewn river on the threshold
the curls of a giantess
past which the sun would penetrate
again and again,
now squeezed out by politicians –

returning I break
bilberries in my mouth,
watch how the sun
lowering by grasses gilds the stone,
makes each stem a wand of light.

Tracks

The hedges
woven nets to hold in land,
the land humming and full,

and I, watching
for sheep, fearing
she would be off like a red fiend –

even in the meadows,
on the high breast of the hill
it becomes harder

to forget the town,
find the narrow way
where all is light, golden,

slow scent and the drone of bees,
to ramparts of gold-cast gorse
holding a little garden.

'Here' say the voices,
'here, in this blaze-rimmed quietness,
here, where there is only flower and wind –'

but they are cutting the woods –
and there is no travelling, only
words, words,

the wet-snouted dogs
and a raven
grunting and circling.

Below, there is
a wide way like a processional,
a track broad enough for three carts –

should I make more of it than that?
More than
beads wound by the old well,

the canoe
at the ceremonial eating place,
a fern uncurling like a heart?

Trucker's Moll

for Michael

> *In the forest without leaves...*
> *Cables for roots,*
> *Thickets of knotted iron, and hard knots of rivets*
> *Swelling in the rain.*
>   John Haines, *The Owl in the Mask of the Dreamer*

I

Two men tend steel leviathans,
easy in flapping shirts and oil-griped slacks,
while a young boy, the owner's son, perhaps,
at home with petrol hose and lengths of rope,
busies himself about the smaller tasks.
Up front, the new machines are glistening and huge;
behind them rusting 'fridges, steel struts.
On the perimeter, trees sway. I lean back, and
the compound dogs watch me coldly for misbehaviour.
When we mount, the cab's curtains are swagged,
tassle-edged, a trucker's home from home.
The engine shivers: we reverse to load machinery.
The stone-grinder for England is a dark hunched lump.

Then out, by dust-limed hedges, houses,
Our Lady Crowned Credit Union, to the by-pass:
his job to haul on the wheel, mine to whisper
propitiatory rhymes to magpies, fill in
the tachograph, the trailer rough-rocking
the tractor unit as I learn to pace the journey,
not ask 'what's next?', take in the wide-angle
shot of mountains, rivers, a cut cornfield,
a boarded-up Protestant church.
He feels the big engine pick up, the swish
of the air brakes; I gaze at deep-uddered cows,
a crow saving grain with one eye on us.
In the fields the corn is hot gold, level-cut.

Gold is the colour of grain, not grain gold,
I learn, as we pull to a yard heaped with it.
Were Midas' stores like this, the seed richer
than the metal? Grain spills from a mechanical shovel,
lies softly mounded, so rich you could live
for ever on it. But the Big House here is gone;
beyond the stone barns rises a newer farmhouse
of concrete blocks. Loading a grain dryer:
by a peeling shed a girl and her grandmother watch.
Men shout commands, heave on ropes,
strain like two steeds perfectly matched;
to participate in this is, for them, heady stuff.

II

As dusk falls by trees that arch for us
at Fermoy, my fingers are salt and chip-oil.
I nurse secret pleasures, anticipate
the Rock of Cashel rearing up, villages
patterning themselves under our height.
We are heading to Belfast, and each landmark
speaks: the Boyne at Drogheda, after Dundalk
the no-man's strip of border, the stain of ghost-
ramps, the long-deserted customs post.
On the MI our shadow under the floodlights
pursues us, catches us, goes past,
and the Kesh glares briefly and is lost to sight.

III

On the Larne boat good Ulsterwomen
are short-haired, bare-faced, decently clad.
A wife wants a dander round. Her husband,
blear-eyed, sulky, refuses. Hiding the banner
of my Southern newspaper, I am soft for the land
that oversaw my birth, finger tartan pens

in the ship's tourist shop. In Scotland everything
is upright as thistles: wall finials, the severely
stepped white gable ends, and black rock;
the black castle staring us out, wet
slate on the roofs in Ballantrae. What
Spartan children play on the grey beach at Girvan?
To sea, huge and faint, a mirage becomes
the hump of Ailsa Craig. Wrack on the beach,
lava cooled to tortuous shapes, the bare
black Calvinist graveyard of Kirkoswald. No king
in Dunfermline, but his children bicker between
the towers of a grey housing estate. I sleep
through Perth, but Dundee, from the by-pass, looks
the same. A Burger King. Some Aberdeen Angus
cattle. We are far north, but the expected Highlands
turn to grain-fields, as the light pales towards dusk
and the straw on the grain-fields turns pearl-white.

IV

A rent in the clouds, then the day appears,
grey, storm-coloured; all the land I cannot
see falls away to either side of us, there is
only tarmac, the hurtling stream of trucks.
Then slow light on the grey-green Border hills,
a castle, sheep-cropped slopes, and woods,
purple willowherb; a church in a sea of it,
a deserted cottage. Our road runs levelly south;
juggernauts cannot have constant
changes on the wheel, changes on the gear lever,
and the flux along black arteries accumulates wealth
for someone with accountants and computers – a long way off.

V

Dark fractured stone makes occasional walls;
climbing the rig bucks and lifts
as the low gears take over; behind us
a place not to be revisited, at least not
until the next trip. And I am at ease,
watching late summer Pennine landscape as stone
turns to peach-gold, sometimes terracotta.
Castles marshal the land: to Roman Britons
this was a frontier wild as the Khyber Pass.
Now ridges of limestone rise and fall like the keys
on a great mechanical organ; now stone declines,
steel rears, it seems from here to London,
Delhi, Shanghai, Chicago. And I have forgotten
the place I came from, the people I left, would
have settled for the shut café in the hills,
but for rumbling, constant as sea, but not soothing.

VI

In the dead heartland of the country we pass
Darlington. Pylons stalk the flat land, their
atrophied arms held out, as electromagnetism
or something spins on the wires, and an intersection
sucks us up, turns us round, shoots us out.
At the low hedge by the entrance to the estate,
a wind-ripped length of plastic flutters.
'Do not enter the crime scene.' What
garish act briefly lit up the unharvested grass,
each huddle of sheds that keep to themselves?
The men who enter do not fear eavesdroppers.

In the noise-racked shed, men lean over steel, adjust
machines. Sparks from an unseen welder's torch
splay on the greasy pavement. The machines hiss
and thump. A forklift comes for the stonecrusher
we have brought from Cork to Gateshead.
Under the rack the forks slide in. The steel
screams. The driver shifts his grip. The metal
screams again then yields as the forklift
takes the six tons easily. Outside there are toy-bright
batterers, shovels, and tubs to break down rock.

He leaves to telephone base. Alone,
in the long side mirrors of the truck,
I am revealed to myself: trucker's moll
in a too-tight top; hair loose, veiling
a weathering face. A moll almost past it?
Dead grass, after the long drought.
South-west, a land of blighted rivers, and iron-
girdered towers, with a grey sky over it.
Proud gardeners, these northern Englishmen:
one man has castellated his hedge. A woman,
grim-faced, negotiates a roundabout; at home
difficult men, hearty talk, as machinery
inexorably razes their jobs. A family, fair,
like they all are here, passes. A politician
on radio chooses the Dead March from Saul,
and two young men, one with a gold earring,
count themselves fortunate to afford a car, cds,
two weeks, perhaps, in Spain or the Algarve.

Smoke coils from towers. I pick at the landscape,
try to make sense of it, listen abstractedly
to the north-of-England talk. We pull
to a truckstop. Inside, a haze of flies,
and men with great golden-haired arms
who lean over shepherd's pie and chips.
Tattoos nestle. The men are intent on cricket;

under the screen a boy rattles a slot machine.
A girl brings them her mother's apple pie
and cream. The apple is innocent of spices.
The skirts of the great chimneys, smoke-tipped:
nine of them I saw, with two smaller, on the bypass
near Leeds. Ubiquitous architecture of stained
concrete, but the voices change: Gateshead
to Manchester to Birmingham; I savour the voices.

VII

After the Forest of Dean, a slow river,
wooded slopes, and church spires pricking
the sky. Each spire is different. This thinning
to tidier Welshness, then to withered hills
and a forest of steel that sprouts smoke. By the river
a tribe of travellers with their wealth of scrap.
Squat churches, signs for 'home cooking' where we cannot
stop, by-roads where we swoop down a slope
and rise heavily up the next, gravity
sticking us to the tarmac. A burnt rubber smell
as we brake for the tightest turn yet;
the cab swings from side to side,
brushing the hedge. At Fishguard I touch rock,
pick blackberries. A butterfly over our cab.
Someone shouts 'Hurry or you'll keep us
all late,' as drivers spill from the rest rooms.
We form a lumbering line to board, low posts
between us and the water as we lurch out and back.

VIII

Ireland: an uncertain quality to the light,
a hovering milkiness. I am revisiting with washed eyes,
as under coverlet of dark the land tucks
itself away, slope by slope. Ragged hedges
under a ragged black sky, a wild oldness –
as time slows, like the old song a singer
has to pace out, and Youghal echoes
our rattling back to us, before we plunge into
the final soft darkness towards Cork.

Men of the South

after Sean Keating's painting in the Crawford Gallery, Cork

Come close enough
you can almost smell
the wet wool of their cloth
as they squat on the damp grass
of a sketched-in mountain slope,
their khaki coats
a preponderance of ochre
under the young, flushed faces,
as fixed on the mid-distance, they wait
for a Crossley tender to appear,
snout first, hugging the bend;
wait to tighten the index finger
and release a fusillade of shots, cracking
the glassy silence of the mountain morning.

It will be all over in seconds.
And we, with our considered morality,
who should we blame?
These young men know no second thoughts:
intent as cats, they do not hear us
tiptoe past in the new century,

their politics outmoded,
their innocence fresh-faced, dangerous.

Rostellan

The two dogs whine –

hush, we will walk
the ghost-laden woods,
take our courage in our hands

walk the ghost-laden
woods of Rostellan,
as thrushes and wood-doves

call between echoing woods.
A blackbird, alarmed, co-corros –
we will not harm you –

the birds fall silent
but the woods are
laden with scent,

and I thought,
why is the way so clear
if not by poisoning?

Not by the hand of dead gardeners,
and these slender trees, singing,
were planted after them.

What is that
gold-flowered, slender-leaved plant?
A gold leaf falls.

The woods hold night still in their branches,
under them is the low broken wall
of a disappeared pleasure garden,

the ruined tower is quiet,
the tide laps shingle
at the sea wall the waves have tunnelled out

and sea-birds cry bitterly – a lament?
'1727' on an embrasure:
then the house had two centuries to stand,

now a solitary pillar, grass-grown,
moss-laden, has a season or two left
before the sea topples it.

I am restless
until the place
gives up its secrets:

here the plough turns worked stone over
and a high wall, hidden by brambles
is easily missed,

as you walk the plot
a fair prospect of the bay opens out,
here where duck rise

great rooms were lit by water-light,
kick at the turf, you will find
bare stone underneath.

Leaving I sought
irrefutable evidence further than the map:
the dark of ancient shrubberies,

an atmosphere so palpable
I could barely speak,
if there had been

anyone to be spoken to,
trotting in an old brougham,
taking the trap to church.

A scent of fox,
the dense brambles weaving to hide –
what? a sleeping city?

The straight path leads on and up:
a sweet chestnut, ringed with sprigs, with rent bark,
and a great oak…

the flowers press on us.
Only for the track we should be lost.
I find raspberries, and Persephone, I eat,

my boots sprout leaves,
a silvery belling from birds' beaks
in the soughing trees,

and everywhere
like carillons of small white bells
enchanter's nightshade.

A shot gun blast, far off.
Would one of the dead gardeners
wonder at the marks I made?

You meet no-one
in the woods of a Sunday dawn.
And, if my pen runs out

a perfect feather,
fresh-fallen, white-edged;
waved it resists the breeze –

still my hunger, and the dogs' hunger
spurs me on;
the shot gun again,

the dogs slower, more deliberate.

Controlling Fire: The Sculpture Factory

The great boat
lit suddenly by welding light
as I pass dockland
to reach the place,

in the mask
it becomes a dim point
cutting steel;

the plasma cutter
drips points of fire
that stab lightly at
my arms, my feet.

Heron

barbed hunter
stalking the mudmarsh
near Ennis

Poet

a whole day
waiting for one word
and then what?

Nunnery

I would retreat
to the nunnery of myself
where thought sprouts
tropically
twining and pressing
so densely I could grow
a whole forest of it;

it might take a year
to tend,
or search a way,
bending branches,
through the thicket
to some kind of clearing.

Like Heloise
I would be enclosed
only might call
softly, sometimes at night,
or creep out
once or twice a year
to discover you.

Revisiting The National Museum, Dublin

The gold garish, incredible,
against the age-blackened heaps
of nuts, of wood, of skin;

the crouching bog man,
his face contorted, agonised,
his cloak sewn hide –

did his paddling tribe
run the Lurgan long-boat
on the inland sea of the North?

Did the great reflector
of the paten
cradle the sun in glory?

– its edge studded with inlay so miniscule
our book-wearied eyes
can scarcely distinguish it.

Skull

Impossible not to be moved
by her curved, weathered skull
half out of the sand
in the half light of evening;
the neck twisted, jaws open,
ghastly and beautiful.
And when her face emerged
gradually from the screen
we knew her instantly,
she was no stranger, but
a lost figure journeying
all the way from the sixth century:
a near neighbour, someone's wife,
as like the living as any one of us.

The Blind Woman

She was the still mentor
of the house,
the hearth goddess.

At first you saw darkness,
then a small figure by the range
feeding the fire,

outside
her brother with sleeves rolled
splitting wood for it.

On The Great Blasket

The weight of stone, salt on my tongue,
as we skim clear water to the landing place;
a rabbit caught in a sheltering hollow
gazes as we gaze back
at the hill holding a honeycomb of fields:
a safe place against wind and wave,
a sheltering fortress;

and something catches my throat
unexpectedly, I have no real link
with the place, have only read,
like the others, the words
that came out of it. Today
a group of children babble
in English, as I choose a track

that rises to the south,
where wind blows up over the cliff
and Iveragh hangs on the horizon,
then take a fine road cut along the slope –
the tawny red of mountain grass
and a little heaven of flowers under my feet.
To be here is to know perfect happiness:

the well dripping from an underhang,
the smooth parchment of the sand
waiting to be written on, the tender
bells of ling. There are stones speckled
with a lacework of lichen,
tufts of sheep's hair among the grass;
I wind a strand, damp and soft, over my palm;

below, the community of huts and fields
is scribed along the slope, the land
man-sculpted, everything proportionate.
A wrinkled sea over the scoop of bay,
the pale mainland, as a gannet drifting overhead
cries, 'Pieu, pieu,' and Brandon blurs,
a black edge of cloud moves from the west…

Storm forecast: the scent of muck,
a tarred roof shivering in the storm light.
The waves, beginning to rise,
eddy and suck at the rock
as we complete our exodus
on the last boat back, perhaps, for days –
the swell grey as slate, becoming deep.

Irish Classes

Buiochas le Dia

We are to thank God
it is a fine day
that I am well
but which?

the god of flags and churches?
the god of plaster
who hangs horribly nailed?
the god who lurks

behind the mission's sombre panelling?
and no cause
to thank him resentfully
as even in English

he is laid in with medieval stitchery:
'Good God!' we say, 'God forbid!'
even the 'God be wi' you'
of goodbye;

which god
we still might lean on in the wind,
sense in the rush of spring water,
when we touch

the flesh warmth of earth;
which god of contrition or compassion,
of time circling or time running
we cannot reach to

and yet may call on at our end.

Infirmary

Through me the way into the suffering city
Dante: Inferno III, 1

I

Needles are pressed
into my inert flesh
as I lie here, labelled
like a newborn.
If I die, at least
they will not lose the body.
Under my curtain
the white feet of nurses pass.

At last I am taken,
turned through a labyrinth
of glass to face
doors which say
'Theatre. Do not enter.'

I enter feet first.
Laid on a slab, it seems
I am the centre
of an obscure ritual.
An anaesthetist chats.
Beyond her two men in green
wash bare arms meticulously.

Am I to be filleted?
This bed is like
the pedestal of tombs
marble figures are laid on.

II

Nora, curled foetally,
is more changeling than
child or woman, as
porridge is spooned
into her bemused
ninety-year old face.

Rose mouths prayers in pain,
'Mary...Sacred Heart...'
shivers, then
pleads for painkillers.
They promise
'the doctor will be round soon.'

I try to put flesh on those
old bones, imagine them
young and lovely:
Iris, Rose Moran,
Nora, Mary Browne...

Firmly, a nurse takes
Mary's flowers. 'Will I
put them by Holy Mary,
by the statue?' Rose's
daughter comes. 'How's Mam?'

III

Morning – the room still dark.
A nurse draws the blinds,
proffers bedpans. Must I be
shameless as the sheela na gig
that grins over the bridge
at Fethard? A river
runs under her splayed legs.

Iris, messenger of the gods
(once a tearaway on horseback)
is scolded by nurses
who do not like
her imperious accent.
She stares ahead, waiting
desperately for a bed pan.

IV

In the new ward I meet
the unblinking gaze of
a little hunched woman.
Next door
an unseen old lady
with nothing more than
'Oh dear. Oh dear dear dear,'
to communicate distress,

and the West Cork
women-talk, 'Ha' ye
microwave?' – keeping
bread in the freezer –
or 'the only thing
you're allowed to kill
nowadays is babies...'

the whispered
gossip of cleaning women.

V

I make an oven
of mashed potato,
rake the inside out,
drink clear water
to take away the taste,

O Cathy – bring me
your fresh-plucked parsley
and your fresh face,
rosy from the wind –

he has not
come to visit yet,
he will arrive
late and penitent, perhaps.

VI

Storm warning:
hollow windsounds
along the pane
as twelve plump-breasted seagulls
rest on the mown grass

and a weary morning nurse:
'Mother of God!
There was no end
to the bedpans
over the last night!'

Sunday ritual: a nurse
carrying a candle, and a monk
with one shoelace undone.
The women bless themselves.
The little procession heads on out.

VII

As well you did not
come in the morning,
everyone would have watched us.

Lunch is at twelve and then
bedpans, so two will be
plenty of time to receive you...

behind a curtain
a woman defecates. I eat
my half slice of white bread,
my half slice of brown bread.

The old lady who walks in her sleep
suddenly rises.
I dream of walking,
every night.

VIII

News. I am to have
a Zimmer frame, in Belfast
the little house flaring
smokestains, its burned windows
boarded up;

The blonde smokes,
sucks her inhaler.
The old ones sleep, snowy
heads on the pale sheets:
their parchment-pale skin.

IX

There is Zimmer frame
burn on my hands.
I count get–well cards.

Must I stay
to know the darkness
under the eyes that means pain,
to speak the words 'help me',
to delight in company again?

or to see
my future in those white heads,
those tremulous hands,
that bare transparent skin.

November

Unsoftened by
summer growth, stones
are grey and pitiless.

Sileage bags
glisten like
black slugs,

berries fade
to the colour of
wine stain, old blood.

Asylum Seekers

We did not meet their eyes,
fearing their ebony faces
might suck us in with a great smile;

so dark,
so deep deep dark
as midnight, as forests;

'coloured' we called them
as though we had
no colour at all, were not pinkish,

or 'black' as if they were not
all browns
from tawny to deepest burnt chocolate,

or the *fir gorm*,
fearing those we were ignorant of –
blue men from the bounds of the Atlas mountains.

Flowers in March

St Patrick's Day, 2003

That evening, for the festivities,
fire flowers bloomed all along the river
orange red crimson
blossoming and shrinking
to splinters high in the night air;

everyone gazed and clapped.
Some stopped their ears but
all were thunderstruck
with delight as they returned
to their suburban homes and flats.

A week later we watched flowers of fire
blossom in another night sky.
Some stopped their ears.
Others, thunderstruck, waited
to see if bombs would fall

like dice, this way or that,
on their flats, their suburban homes
in the cities of Iraq.

A Day at the Zoo

Look – there are humans
between the penguins and the marmosets;
there, in that kiosk, where a girl

hands ice-cream and drinks
to those who cannot wait for
the restaurant at the end of the track,

and there, more, whooping
at the frenzied gibbon till he whoops back,
and there, by the lake,

a little boy throws stones at ducks,
and a toddler, unchided, chases
a marsupial with sad dark eyes.

The cheetahs turn their backs on us.
The eagle, tattered as a feather duster,
gazes seawards over the mud flats;

a last herd of scimitar oryx graze,
wondering who had changed
Arabian skies for Irish.

Cut-backs: no-one has given fresh leaves
to the giraffes, they strain down for grass;
the rest of the island's sold for a golf course.

Swansea Activity Pack

for Robert

'A fine day', I said.
'If it lasts', she replied, snatching my cup.
In the heart of Wales it is
Raining. Tidy your room. Have another turn.
Late for your evening meal at the guest house. Go back to start.

An exciting day sailing in Swansea Bay.
Land stretched to the sea, would have swallowed it.
Spend a day on the beach.
A little girl on the beach in a red dress, dancing
the rat and carrot, hat and tarot...

The man who fears butterflies sleeps.
Fall asleep. Throw 1, 3 or 6 before you can move.
In the Seychelle Guest House
the whisper of palm fronds, in the glass-house
the spined columns of desert plants.

Caught in a downpour. Shelter.
Miss a turn. In the café
the hatstands are festooned
with macs and walking sticks.
A Welsh maiden and biros for everyone.

Ceri Hughes Ls Paul Watkins.
He has gone to the Air Force Recruiting Office.
She peers at the ejected cockpit seat,
the mannequin whose face is peeling,
whose plaster nose is chipped –

A flying lesson at Swansea Airport.
The plane lurched, banked, rose
to twenty-four thousand feet.
Through the rain there is
peace, light of sun on the face.

Pony Trekking. Throw twice.
On the heathy plains of Gower there are horses.
The slow, ferny slope.
There is a hole at the Point of Worme Heade,
but few dare enter into it –

the stumps of the wrecked boat
rear from the sand.
Your boat in the Marina needs repair. Miss a turn.
At the Head the Worm roars, lashing its tail.
They are leaving the Chapel. Do they hear it?

The War

Hush. I will not tell them
you are growing furiously, silently,
from the stump they cut last year,
your stalks healing bare pipes and concrete

with green shade. In the grey city
every green spear is a guerrilla fighter
hissing freedom. Your shoots thrust out
dangerously, everywhere you erect

leafy receptors to power your takeover;
showers fuel you as you crawl,
bladed, armed, over rooftops,
across dusty terrain, firing

sudden pollen, an intermittent
but deadly bombardment of seed.
Bees drone overhead, your agents;
birds swiftly drop your grenades.

You never rest. If we rest you are
up and away, our apparent victory
is temporary. And we are deaf
to your troop movements,

do not know from which corner
your next attack will be –
still we tear you from roots,
shrivel you with lethal fluid

and you appear to melt away, leaving
tangible corpses by the roadside,
then come at us from another angle.
The force is with your ragged troops,

I will defect to your side,
leave my garden to wilderness,
don a bandolier of seed,
with my breath spray dandelion

to the four winds, scatter
moss spores into concrete.
There is grain hidden in my pocket:
from the dry pods new green will grow.